MW00424989

Mario Lopez

How I Know

A Story to Strengthen Your Faith

MARIO LOPEZ WITH DANIELLE LOPEZ

WESTBOW
PRESS®
A DIVISION OF THOMAS NELSON
& ZONDERVAN

Scripture quotations are taken from the Holy Bible, New Living
Translation, copyright ©1996, 2004, 2007, 2013, 2015 by Tyndale
House Foundation. Used by permission of Tyndale House Publishers,
Inc., Carol Stream, Illinois 60188. All rights reserved.

WestBow Press books may be ordered through
booksellers or by contacting:

WestBow Press
A Division of Thomas Nelson & Zondervan
1663 Liberty Drive
Bloomington, IN 47403
www.westbowpress.com
1 (866) 928-1240

ISBN: 978-1-5127-7685-0 (sc)
ISBN: 978-1-5127-7684-3 (e)

Print information available on the last page.

WestBow Press rev. date: 07/25/2017

For my children. May you allow Christ to reign in your heart and strengthen you with the power of His Holy Spirit.

Contents

Contents

CHAPTER 1

❧ ❦ ❧

An Awakening

I came to gasping, sweating, shaking, crying, and repeating, "It's all true! It's all true!"

My mother was by my hospital bedside crying tears of joy when she realized—yet again— that her son would live to see another day. Unfortunately, this was not my first brush with death, or hell for that matter. I'd been blown up, crushed, and burned alive before this last near-death experience. However, it was during this experience, as I lay in my hospital bed with a temperature of 108°, that I saw for a second time what awaited me on the other side. I decided to get serious about surrendering my life to the Savior.

It is becoming increasingly difficult for people to acknowledge that there is a Creator of this universe, this planet, and what we call life. To many, it is even more preposterous to suggest that there would be *only one* path to knowing that Creator. In a post-Darwinian era, people are highly skeptical of the possibility of a supernatural being intervening in their lives—a being they could one day be accountable to for the choices they made.

In America, we currently face a growing trend of people who believe in a relativistic view of morality and truth. *Who is to say what is right, wrong, or true?* We certainly are at a crossroads in our culture—*if there is no such thing as truth, why bother living a certain way? Why bother doing the right thing?* Those who say there is no God usually take a position of moral relativism, where there are no absolutes. *What is wrong in one culture can be right in another. What I believe to be true is true for me, despite being contrary to evidence, and that's okay.*

The constant bombardment of our brains with overwhelming amounts of information and misinformation can make it almost impossible for one to discern what is true. *How can one be certain that one knows there is life after the physical body dies? How can one know that there is one true God?* After a series of supernatural experiences and moments where I've faced my own mortality, and through my own multidisciplinary study, I have concluded that I *know* there is one true God. My name is Mario Lopez, and like many people, I have a story to tell. I like to call this story—the story of "How I Know."

CHAPTER 2

Old Life

When I was young, I thought I knew what life and God were all about. In my high school years, I was what many Christians would refer to as a "worldly" person.

The Bible cautions against worldliness:

> Do not love this world nor the things it offers you, for when you love the world, you do not have the love of the Father in you. For the world offers only a craving for physical pleasure, a craving for everything we see, and pride in our achievement and possessions. These are not from the Father, but are from this world. (1 John 2:15–16 NLT)

As Christians, it is often said that we are to be in the world but not of the world. As human beings, in our nature, at our core, we are tied in many ways to the comforts, sensations, and temptations of this world. We often make decisions based on what will bring us the most pleasure and what will cause us to avoid pain. I was more interested in living life on my own terms. My parents, however, attempted to mold me into someone I really didn't understand—a Christian.

I was sent to private school and completely sheltered from R rated movies and worldly music about sex and drugs. My biological parents divorced when I was very young. Every other weekend I had the opportunity to escape from my overly Christian, sheltered world and get a taste of the "good life," or so I thought. I had one foot in the world and the other in the church. I knew what was outside of the Christian home, and I anxiously awaited my moments of opportunity to break free from rules and oppression enforced by this God I didn't know and His Bible.

In my infinite teenage wisdom, I secretly thought that my overly Christian parents had no clue about what the world had to offer. *How could enjoying some music, some edgy movies, or a few alcoholic drinks here and there be so bad?* In my opinion, my parents got it all wrong and needed to just loosen up! After all, God made us to enjoy life! Right? Yes! Enjoyment would be part of this life but not all of it. God's idea of enjoying life is also different from the world's view of enjoying life.

The things I thought were enjoyable then— in the long run—only brought me and others pain. When I was living for my own pleasure, I couldn't see that my parents were trying to protect me from destruction and deception. Like many high school–age teens, I went my own way. I did what seemed right in my own eyes, regardless of the values my parents tried to instill in me. Much of my focus was on my social life and relationships. Ultimately, I became a father my senior year in high school. I knew things had to change and change rapidly. I now needed to provide a future for this little life I had created.

CHAPTER 3

Motivated

I joined the US Army Reserves. Shortly after I went on active duty, I received notice that I was being sent to Iraq. My worldview was rather limited then. I rarely left the great state of Texas and didn't know much about life except earning a living and being a family man. I often joke that Iraq was my "college experience." To me, as a young person, it was actually a breath of fresh air. No more pressure of being the head of the household; my new job was to be a full-time soldier. My focus was my country, my duty, and my physical wellbeing.

*2003 marked the beginning of
my new life in the military.*

Being a new father was not my only motivation to serve in the military. I remember being in my second-period class watching television as it showed images of a building billowing with smoke. I heard someone say on the news that a plane hit one of the twin towers of the World Trade Center in New York City.

I thought for a second, *Wow, who could make such a dumb mistake?* Then a second plane hit. I came to realize that what I was observing was not a mistake but a planned terrorist attack. At that time, I could not come to terms with what had just happened. It seemed like hundreds of questions bombarded my mind all at the same time: *What does this mean? What are we going to do? Will this be our new normal? Will there be more of these attacks? If so, where? Will our country become another hotbed of terrorist activities, like Iran or Palestine? Is this the end of the world?*

It seemed the only answer I got from television, friends, family, and my own immature logic was revenge. Maybe something in my brain was filtering their replies, and all I heard was revenge. I know this thinking sounds a bit much for the average seventeen-year-old to conclude, but I can remember clearly the comments I made to people around me. When we went to invade Iraq, I told one of my teachers, "I should be out there." She tried to make me promise not to ever join the service. We all know how that ended.

CHAPTER 4

℀

Desert Life

Once my squad got settled in Iraq, we began our regular mission and going "out the wire," which means off our base and out among the local population. I began to feel compassion for the people and their children, who looked so much like me and my children. Whenever I had the opportunity, while driving past the little ones, I found myself throwing them candy and MRE goodies out of the truck windows. It was as though I was a character on a parade float. I loved my job as part of an engineering company in Iraq, clearing roads and making safe passageways for the rest of the boys.

My first day In Afghanistan, awaiting the Chinook to transport us to our destination.

Preparing to roll out on mission in Afghanistan.

While on duty we worked hard, and off duty we played hard too. There were pools and lakes, long bike rides, and of course—the gym—which we referred to as "the temple." This is where I spent most of my downtime.

Some days we could enjoy movies, and we ate some pretty good food on base. Thanks to the American taxpayers, we were treated with steak and shrimp on Fridays! These comforts of home really helped boost morale while we were away from our beloved country.

However, one of the most encouraging things I personally witnessed was the Iraqis voting. I really believed we were helping to spread freedom and democracy. The fruits of our labor seemed evident, and it appeared that our sacrifice was not in vain. My Platoon Sergeant used to say, "Soak it up boys 'cuz it'll never be this good on deployment again!" I felt blessed, but I didn't truly understand his words until a year and a half later when we deployed to Afghanistan.

I write my experiences of this deployment with heaviness in my spirit. I was in love with the military until Afghanistan. Afghanistan was a pit of desolation, and I had an eighteen-month deployment to look forward to. Here we did not witness the citizens participating in a democratic process. Here the infrastructure we were building, would be wiped away with the next sandstorm. Sand was everywhere and in everything. This sand was not like the sand on our beloved Texas coast—it was fine and powdery. And although we had never seen dust on the moon, that's exactly what we called it— moon dust. The air was hot, our base was hot, our living quarters were hot, and the drinking water was always hot, as long as I was there anyway. No more steak Fridays in Afghanistan!

In Afghanistan I had enemies around every corner. One of the US Army's purposes for being there was to train Afghani men to help build their Afghani army, which would allow them to protect their own land from the Taliban once the United States withdrew. Unfortunately, we continued to train this new army despite knowing that Taliban operatives had infiltrated. While out on mission, sometimes we slept in a courtyard of the Afghani army base. We had our guns mounted in front to protect us while we slept. The only problem was that sometimes our protection—an Afghani trainee—was asleep too! I quickly learned that while on one particular base, I needed to position myself in a corner and protect myself as best as I could from being a soft target.

Unfortunately, nothing was done to change our dangerous sleeping arrangements. I had to count on myself and my own instincts for survival. Imagine enemies all around you, and you are at their mercy. I had guys I couldn't trust behind me—the Afghani Army—and Taliban operatives capable of walking right into our vehicle staging and camping area. I slept very lightly. I kept my knife unsheathed and a round in my weapon, just in case.

A long four months into my deployment, our squad ran over an improvised explosive device (IED). The short mission I was expecting turned out to be the longest, most difficult mission of my life. They say hindsight is twenty-twenty. Now as I look back, I can see that we were sitting ducks. Weeks prior to the attack on my truck, there was another platoon of soldiers who were hit with an IED while on mission.

It is my understanding that the Taliban hit the first and the last vehicles in the convoy of three trucks, thereby sandwiching a vehicle in the middle. Apparently, the men operating the middle truck assessed that it was better to hightail it out of the situation. Unfortunately, after the Criminal Investigation Department (CID) was called in, it was discovered that a survivor was left behind.

The CID surmised that Taliban operatives must have investigated the wreckage and pulled out the survivor. Unfortunately what CID did not yet know was that the operatives had already beheaded the survivor and took the body with them to their village to collect a reward for their kill. Soldiers have a bounty on their head. According to the rules these men played by, the higher the rank of the soldier, the more money they received for their kill. When CID determined their might be a survivor, they presented their findings to the commander and he decided to surround the village with troops, find out what happened, and find our soldier—dead or alive.

The commander achieved all his objectives and was able to simultaneously apprehend a couple of top terrorist leaders. Sadly, he also found that the surviving soldier's remains were mutilated and buried in an unmarked grave in the moon dust outside a house in the village. On a bittersweet note, the commander ordered the remains of the brave soldier recovered and sent home so our guy could have the hero's ceremony he deserved.

Needless to say, the Taliban had some revenge to take up with us, as well as the local population. Like little children, they threw a fit and sent their minions to destroy the infrastructure we had built, including blowing up surrounding bridges, which the villagers benefited from. That's where I came in. I was stationed in an engineering company. We were nicknamed "Earth movers." We cleared paths to make ways around the bridges so that the local population could live their lives in the mist of this never-ending war.

We positioned our gun trucks to provide security and got to work moving earth, clearing paths, and building. While working on these roads, it wasn't strange to accumulate a traffic jam of fifty or sixty buses—mini trucks with all kinds of exotic produce, and vans full of people. In America, we also experience this when construction is under way, a classic rush-hour scene in the big city, except this one was in the middle of the dessert. Women were covered from head to toe. Their only visible accessories were children close by clinging onto them. It was an interesting paradox for me to see young Afghani boys clinging and adoring their mothers, then see the adult Afghani males who appeared to dismiss their female partners.

Back to the desert traffic jam. There were people camping alongside the road, waiting for a path to be cleared. I found it odd that it never occurred to some of these people to use a little problem solving and go around all the mess if they really needed to get by. Sure, it wasn't the most pleasant trip through the sand, but at least they could move along with the business they had to attend. Vehicles would break down from time to time in the sand. I could not just stand idly by when the Afghani people got stuck. I lent a helping hand by pushing their vehicles out of the dust.

While this was happening, I wondered if we US soldiers looked like super humans to them. As soon as one of us got to a stalled vehicle, we helped push them along—no matter how many were inside. I also wondered if I ever rubbed shoulders with my attempted murderer—the soldier poacher who placed the bomb on the road, the one who pushed the detonator that fateful day. I say murderer because I, Mario Lopez, am no longer the Mario Lopez I used to be. Some may say I changed for the better, however I admit I'm neutral on the matter. I have lost much, but I have gained much also.

*Images of my vehicle being assessed
and preparing for transport
after the IED attack.*

CHAPTER 5

🜚 ◎ 🜚

A Journey Begins

There are so many strange variables that led to this new life. It really does appear as though it was a perfectly orchestrated cosmic set up. Did the fortunate and unfortunate circumstances come from above or below? The verdict is still out. I'm just glad that being blown up was the catalyst that led me into a relationship with the true author and finisher—Jesus Christ. The life I live today is so much more than I could have ever imagined. In the Bible, there is a promise for all believers:

> And we know that God causes everything to work together for the good of those who love God and

are called according to his purpose
for them. (Romans 8:28 NLT)

On August 13, 2008, I woke up with a knot
in my stomach. I felt nauseated and anxious. My
platoon sergeant even took notice and offered
me the opportunity to stay behind. It wasn't like
me to take a day off, so I went ahead anyway.
We all climbed inside the truck and planned to
make our short half-day journey to the nearest
base.

I had made this trip dozens of times before
without personal incident; harm always
happened to someone else, never to me. That
day my luck ran out. We made it to what I
believed was just an hour into the trip. There
we were sitting in the back of the truck, knee
to knee with our battle buddies, just passengers
looking around, laughing, and talking when …
boom! The next thing I saw was a gray blanket
covering inside and outside the truck. I felt
weightless as our truck slowly lifted off the
ground and then within seconds came crashing
down back to earth … *bam*! I was knocked
unconscious!

When I woke up, what had just happened

was like a dream. This never could happen to me. I thought, *Just in case this isn't a dream, I should probably do something.* I tried to get up. It was then I realized I was buckled in and my right arm was pinned down. I saw and smelled the smoke; later came the flames. Our medic was also in the truck with me. On our ride, she was right in front of me before the blast. Now she was to the right of me covered with our bags, cocooned from the flames, and screaming for help!

The truck's fuel tank was severed in half and had spilled diesel on the ground. All the kinetic energy from the blast and the flammable debris in the flames met the diesel, and some of it was on me. As I was under the flames, I thought I was a goner. I was on fire, and I had nine 203 grenade launcher rounds strapped to my chest. If you're not familiar with the 203 round, it is like a huge shotgun shell that is not filled with lead but with explosives. I looked up toward the heavens through the pile of metal that was once a MRAP truck, and then everything turned white.

I cried out to God and said, *All right, Jesus, I am coming to meet you!* Nothing else mattered— not my excruciating pain from the blast, not the inferno, not my family, not my mission, not my revenge, nothing. It was a very intimate three-way conversation—me, death, and God. God said no! Death had to obey, and I came back to reality and realized that the little grenades that were strapped to my chest did not go off. I saw boots and hands reaching for me. I was stuck, but that didn't stop them. I warned them I could blow at any moment, but that didn't stop them either. They rescued me out of the clutches of the MRAP of flames. I immediately saw my arm was badly maimed. They then set me on the ground to begin the work of saving my life.

My fellow soldiers managed to pull out the medic, from what I remember, who was unscathed by the flames, and set her down beside me, injured ankles and all.

At first she said, "I can't do this. I can't do this."

She must have been in a great deal of pain and in shock because of what she had just experienced. She almost met her end also. Believe it or not, I still had my wits about me enough to encourage her to get started. I asked her to recall the first steps to evaluating a casualty.

"What's the first step?" I asked. "Breathing. I'm breathing, right, because I'm talking to you. Okay what's the next one? Bleeding. Okay, now stop my bleeding."

Like being set to autopilot, she began her work. "Am I going to die?," I asked.

She looked down at me like I had asked the most ridiculous thing. "You're not going to die!" She chuckled.

Her answer gave me hope.

Soon after the bleeding was stopped, I asked her for some morphine, but she said the medics from the base we had just left would not let her have any. The morphine was being rationed because so many others were injured from attacks such as this one. I was out of luck until help arrived. I laid there in the desert, naked, burned, and battered—the sun beating down on me.

It took the longest forty-five minutes of my life for the helicopter to arrive. When I heard the bird, it was like a heavenly orchestra performing in my heart, knowing there would be a way out. I now felt I had a fighting chance of survival. The air blowing down from the propellers gave me great relief, as it fanned its wind onto my exposed, blistering skin.

They loaded me up on the helicopter and once again, as soon as I could, I asked for morphine. This time I was rejected by the medic because I had lost too much blood. But I was determined to get relief no matter what the cost. I screamed, "I have suffered enough. You will give me morphine!" The medevac medic, seeing I would not take no for an answer, talked it over with his captain and reluctantly conceded. "Okay. It's your funeral," he said, staring down at me through his helmet—a bug like visage.

I imagined he had a slight smirk on his face while he administered a chemical that made it all seem bearable. I don't really remember if he smirked or not. I just remember perceiving a detachment from every medical personnel type that was involved in my treatment. It was as though I was their job, a project, their mission. Maybe I was detecting their sense of relief that it was not them on their deathbed. They had this uncanny ability to remove themselves from the situation like a machine and just get to work. It's what they were trained to do. It's exactly what I needed I guess.

I woke up in a field hospital with doctors asking me questions. I laid on the metal table as they prodded around, searching for ruptures, projectiles, internal bleeding, and so on. While they worked, I remember being asked questions such as, "Who are you? Who is the president of the United States?" I suppose I gave all the correct responses and perhaps even said something humorous because I remember them laughing. I recall a doctor looking at me and saying, "All right, we are putting you back under with some medication. You're headed home."

What a sweet sound to my ears! I felt my body surrender—I was now at their mercy. All that mattered was that I wasn't in Afghanistan anymore. My new existence for the next two weeks would be an intravenous, medically induced coma.

CHAPTER 6

Physical Healing

I don't remember anything while I was in the coma—just blackness, no dreams, and no memories. I was flown across countries, over the Atlantic Ocean, completely unconscious, to Brooke Army Medical Center (BAMC), a premier burn hospital in San Antonio, Texas. Approximately the same time I was being transported, my family was alerted of the situation.

Thankfully, all of them lived just hours away from San Antonio. There are two very well-known military-affiliated hospitals that handle traumatic burns, one in San Antonio and the other in Washington, DC. It's really a blessing that my family is from South Texas and could be there. Many of my friends in the burn unit were from different states. Therefore their families were uprooted to come down to Texas.

The real pain began about a month into my treatment. The doctors began releasing the reins the drugs had on me, and I finally started dreaming again. I started interacting with others around me. They were no longer just faceless phantoms that made things happen around me. I became self-aware and at times, very expressive.

With consciousness came pain. To live in this world there was pain, and in my case, a whole lot of it. It hurt just to breathe. It hurt to move. It hurt to think. My body had all its alarms going off at once. I was hungry but couldn't eat, was thirsty and couldn't drink, my skin itched and burned, my stomach ached, and my brain hurt from all the drugs.

It would be three weeks until the feeding tube and tracheotomy were removed before I could taste the cool moisture of water swirling in my mouth, passing down my esophagus, and into my belly. Oh, the things we take for granted when we are well.

*I was so thankful to see
their smiling faces.*

My family met me at the hospital. I was so glad to see them all once again. I would not have made it without them. Seeing my children's sweet faces bolstered my resolve to stay alive. Having my parents, brother, and sisters there throughout the recovery was truly a blessing. I had so many visitors—Hollywood personalities, military leaders, ministers, founders of nonprofit organizations, and the list goes on! Today I still run into people all over Texas who will tell me, "I was praying for you!" It's amazing! I had some outstanding medical care, but there are some things that even my doctors were baffled by.

Looking back, I'm convinced my recovery was expedited supernaturally by the Lord. We were told I could be in the intensive care unit (ICU) for six months, but I was there for about six weeks. Within two and a half months after leaving the ICU, I was stabilized enough to move out of the hospital and onto living quarters just outside the hospital. For the next three months, I continued rehab and more surgeries. I had to learn how to talk, walk, and feed myself all over again, but now without the use of my right arm or the fingers on the remainder of my left hand.

The road to recovery was still very long. For the next two years, I would continue to undergo surgeries to rebuild my nose and the skin around my right eye, my lips, and skull. Laser treatments relieved tension from the painful scarring. One of my surgeries was done to give me the ability to flex what remained of my thumb and index finger. This surgery was essential to me enjoying the independence I have today. I'm so grateful! Without it there would be no driving, brushing my own teeth, painting, hunting, feeding myself—I could go on and on.

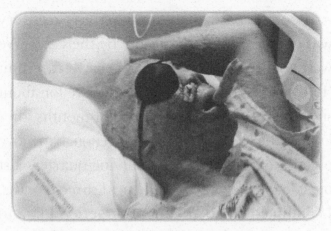

Recovering after one of my many surgeries.

After the surgery was completed on my left hand, I was overjoyed. I could finally feed myself again! My favorite foods were items I could now easily pick up, such as pizza, tacos, and my favorite—burgers. The burgers served two functions; they were easy for me to hold, and they helped me to stretch the skin around my mouth. The burns and reconstruction around my mouth made the opening much smaller than before. All the burgers have helped me to stretch that skin. Well, that's my excuse anyway.

I kept getting a reoccurring infection in my right foot, and believe it or not, they wanted to take that too, but we fought and my family prayed. Thank God the wound healed and my foot didn't have to be amputated. I also had a surgery to make the tendon flexible enough so I did not have to walk like I had a wooden peg for a leg.

In addition to the physical agony, I was experiencing a new world of emotional and mental anguish. I had to adjust to this new person I saw in the mirror. I couldn't work with my hands anymore and do all the activities I once loved. To make matters more complicated, I was facing losing my kids once again, this time to divorce. The depression and anxiety from this perfect storm left me really doubting God.

CHAPTER 7

※ ❀ ☞

Losing Faith

I thought, *How could all this stuff happen to me? Why was I allowed to get blown up? I was a good person.* My parents are ministers, and I was a churchgoer almost all my young life. *He was supposed to protect me!* I came to the realization that I had been a false convert since childhood. All the time I spent in church professing to be a Christian, my heart was stone.

A person with a truly touched heart for Jesus would care to read God's word. They would feel remorse for foul language and would probably not lie deliberately. One who genuinely was touched by the power of the gospel would squirm in his or her seat if he or she chose to watch an R-rated movie or listen to sexually and violently charged mainstream music. Most of all, a born-again Christian would not completely put God on the back shelf of his or her life like I did. I put the doctors, psychologists, and social workers where God should have been—in a high place of reverence, trusting them with my life, and putting hopes for my future in them.

I did everything they asked and completely put my faith in them. The doctors had my trust, and they gave me strength. They took away my anxieties, and the drugs took away my pain. I turned to drinking and self-medicating. I had access to a smorgasbord of chemical candy—Vicodin, morphine, clonazepam, Percocet, gabapentin, and tramadol—but I loved Benadryl. Benadryl soothed the burn of my inflamed skin and made my body feel tingly, cool, and fuzzy all over. The pills relaxed my mind and knocked me out. I took my daily medication cocktail to sooth my pain.

One night in particular, I settled in for bed. I chuckled and thought to myself, *Whoa, I took way too much today.* I was nervous because I knew I might not wake up. I could feel my heart slowing and warm waves flow over me. I gave in to the medication and thought, *If I die, I die. So be it. If there is a God, I deserve to go to heaven. The sacrifices*

I have made for my country constitute a pass to paradise. I felt better after telling myself that.

I am not sure if what happened next was a vision, a dream, or an actual visit to Hell. Although I do know what followed kick started a series of events that lead to my surrender to Christ. That night I woke up and saw my spirit; it looked like smoke after blowing out a candle. *Where am I?* I wondered. I felt that I was traveling downward. As I sank, I saw an orange, glowing pinhole of light—it grew larger as I got closer and closer. The next thing I knew, I hit the floor, and from what I saw and felt all around me—I knew this was not going to be a pleasant experience.

CHAPTER 8

❧ ❧
The First Visit

W hen I hit the ground, I landed on my feet. I looked around and saw a fog in the air. Something in my spirit told me the fog was hate. Hate was a tangible object—I could grab it or bottle it if I wanted to. The best way to describe the feeling of hate was as though you've walked into a room and felt that the person(s) in that room were mad at you for some reason. Here that feeling was multiplied a million times worse! The hate alone was draining, taking life away from me. It was horrible! The hate, believe it or not, was the worst sensation!

Then the next sensation I felt was the heat! The heat was so very strong. It was like nothing I'd felt before. I know what being burned alive on earth feels like. On earth, the flames feel the way they look as they dance on a log. On one's skin the flames jump around as well as the pain; it hurts here and there and at varying intensities on different areas of the body. The flames I felt in this place were all encompassing, maybe how acid would feel, as it hurts all over the body equally at the same time. The burning sensation I felt in hell was much more intense. When I was trapped and being burned alive, oddly enough I started to feel a cooling sensation. I'm sure a rush of endorphins kicked in, but at the same time my nerves were being damaged and I couldn't feel the burning as it was happening— but in the vision of hell it never stopped.

The third sensation I felt was an intense feeling of hopelessness. I can imagine I would feel that hopeless if I got pulled over by a policeman, while speeding in a stolen car, with pounds of drugs in the front seat, a dead body in the trunk, and warrants for my arrest in the system. Surely I would be put away for a very, very long time, without a chance for release, and rightfully so. Of the three sensations I felt, the hopelessness was the least intense. Perhaps the intensity was dulled by my accepting that

I deserved to be there. Thank God I can only remember three sensations.

In my feeling of despair, I looked up to view my surroundings. I observed that I was in a house with no roof, but there were windows. I looked out the window and saw a hurricane of fire blowing in the distance, and through the gusting wind, I saw houses tumbling like tumbleweeds. I was not alone in this house without a roof. I looked around to see hellish creatures staring at me and laughing. It was as though they were enjoying my horror and surprise.

They were all different statures and forms. Some looked like insects, and some looked almost humanoid. One in particular reminded me of a gargoyle perched high, gazing down upon a woman who was levitating on an altar. To me, she looked ancient, a reanimated corpse over hundreds of years old. Her veins were visible through her wrinkled skin, she was mostly bald with patches of white hair, and she was wearing only a black sackcloth gown. The perched, gargoyle-like entity basically pulled me, without ever touching me, to the levitating lady. As he pulled me toward her, I sensed that he wanted me to perform some kind of perverse act with her. I snapped awake as soon as I found myself standing before her. I woke up crying and sick to my stomach because I knew I had just visited a forbidden place not meant for us.

A rendering of what I observed during my first vision of what awaited me after death.

I want you to know that it was very difficult to write this down. Right this very moment I feel weak. The experience of feeling life slipping from my body and seeing the eternity that awaited me was a defining moment, from which my spiritual journey would begin. Looking for an explanation, I sought the guidance of my doctors, psychologist, and social workers. I asked them to help me make sense of what I recently saw and felt. The consensus was that this episode was nothing more than a symptom related to some post-traumatic stress syndrome (**PTSS**) that I acquired from my injury. Without any resistance, I accepted the diagnosis and went about my life the same exact way—still self-medicating and still trying to find pleasure in the things of this world.

CHAPTER 9

The Second Visit

About a year and a half after this experience, I was exploring the prospect of undergoing yet another surgery to reconstruct my face. The procedure involved inserting an implant below the layer of skin in my lower back. Over time, once the skin was stretched, it would be removed and the material used to smooth out and fill in tissue lost on the right side of my face. Usually my surgeries were carried out at BAMC. However, this particular time I was outsourced to a civilian doctor who specialized in these implants. I went in for my scheduled procedure, and the implant was inserted. It was supposed to be an outpatient procedure. When I was released, I was to go back to BAMC to make sure the procedure went well and receive clearance.

Thankfully, my dad came to see me through this procedure. I remember being in the car, leaning forward in pain, and repeating, "Something is not right." He rushed me to the hospital as fast as he could. My military doctors determined that there was some internal bleeding. They decided to administer blood, hoping the bleeding from the surgery would stop. Four pints of blood later, the bleeding persisted. By this time, my mother had arrived to relieve my dad. I was rushed back to the original civilian doctor so the implant could be removed.

I began to experience a transfusion reaction, and my body reached a temperature of 108°. I vaguely remember nurses rushing to place cool towels and icepacks on my overheating body. My veins collapsed, and my body was convulsing. My mother, a minister, called my dad and told him to turn back around. They were losing me again, and this might be good-bye. She began praying intensely and interceding on my behalf. While all of this was going on, suddenly the room became silent, and the nurses, the doctors, and my mother disappeared. The only body in the room was mine, but there were three other entities.

This time there was a gorgeous female, a huge rock form, and a classic devil-looking character. This time the female in the room was calling the shots. She was gorgeous, like a Hollywood actress. The only problem—her skin was green. She wore a revealing, black, sticky garment. Something in my spirit discerned that she was a demon of lust. As she walked, a trail of black goo oozed onto the floor. I believe she embodied the nature of lust as once someone is caught in it, it is very hard to get away. This sin is very enticing, and not many will find the strength to be completely set free.

The second entity in the room was a huge, rock-like, male figure. He looked like something out of a comic book story. Huge and stony, he was a massive obstacle—possibly a demon of pride. The other devil-like character crouched and hopped about almost like a monkey. He was sitting on my chest staring into my eyes. He was looking for signs of life. He took his monkey-like fist and knocked on my forehead as if to ask, "Is there anyone home?" These entities reminded me of the words in 1 John 2:16.

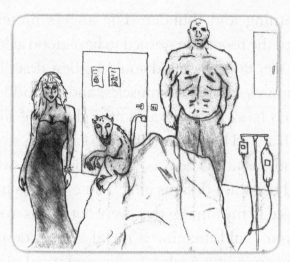

*The entities I observed in my
hospital room as I felt life
slipping from me once again.*

Once again there was a look of pleasure as they gazed upon my suffering. Without moving their lips, they uttered curses at me and cheered, confident that this time they would get to take me to hell with them. They mocked me and reminded me that I had not learned anything from the previous experience. They were satisfied that I did not take the first spiritual encounter seriously.

Just then, the whole ceiling began to morph, and one section began to spin, appearing as a small tornado. Out of the tornado came an angel of God crashing into the room like lightning and thunder. The angel's presence filled the room. He seemed to have stood at least ten feet tall! His build could be best described as muscles on top of muscles, and he had long blond hair. He wore armor of glistening silver with a gold border, and he also carried a sword almost as tall as he was. The blade of the sword had beautiful designs in it. Those designs have stayed in my mind—they were out of this world! If you could imagine a metal web of designs from antiquity: Arabic, Celtic, and tribal swirls, geometric shapes, designed by the mind of a humanly and heavenly creative individual.

That sword was a significant part of what I remember from the vision. As a soldier, I am interested in guns. I didn't know much about swords, so I decided to look up why a sword would have holes inside the blade. From what I read, I learned that the sword could be just as strong but lighter for swiftly moving in battle. According to the Bible, in Ephesians 6:17, the sword represents the word of God. To the Christian it is a mighty weapon of the spiritual kind. The angel appeared in the room with his sword already drawn, held in his hand, pulled up high toward the enemy. He targeted the largest demon in the room, the one that appeared as a huge rock in bodily form—the pride demon.

Suddenly all the spiritual entities were gone. I snapped out of my near-death experience, and the room became "normal." I was perfectly alert. I began describing to my mother everything I just witnessed and confessed to her that I absolutely, urgently needed to make things right with God. She led me in a prayer. It was the first step I took in my journey to find truth in this existence we call life!

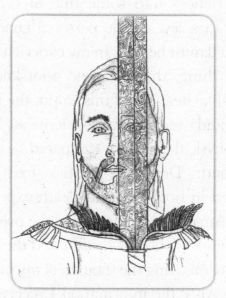

A rendering of the angel who intervened and the weapon he carried.

CHAPTER 10

⊙⊛⊙

Truth

Icould only try to fit my supernatural experiences into some line of reasoning. I came to a few simple personal conclusions: First: Hell must be real. In my experience, I saw and felt things that I had no prior knowledge of (acid-like heat not of this world, the tangible hatred, and the crippling hopelessness). Nothing in my physical existence compared.

Second: Demonic entities exist. They appeared in both my near-death experiences. Third: Angels must exist. I had the privilege of seeing one in action as he attacked the demons who were enjoying the thought of my imminent demise. Also, the information I received from studying the angel's sword alone was full of things I had not known. Fourth: Witnessing both evil and good spiritual beings, I concluded there must be a place each kind would reside— heaven and hell. Finally, the creator of these entities and these places—God—must be real, and I would much rather be with Him than apart from Him.

After I left the hospital, I started searching for some evidence of the supernatural hand of God. For years and years in school, through media and movies, I was told that the world and all that is in it could be explained by some natural law or process. The big bang can explain how matter, the universe, and all the heavenly bodies within came to be, and evolution can explain how all life arose. Biochemistry and evolution can explain thoughts and behaviors. Things seemingly supernatural are mere coincidences or can be explained within some law of physics.

For years and years at home and in church, I was told God said, "Let there be," and the universe, the planet, life, and human consciousness, all had their beginning. The supernatural interventions of an omniscient, omnipotent, loving God orchestrated life in the heaven and on earth. His interaction is not coincidental; it is deliberate!

So which was true? That is what I was searching for—truth. I learned truth is exclusive. Truth cannot deny itself. It cannot contradict itself. It's a basic rule of logical debate. There cannot be a God and not be a God at the same time.

I learned that the theory of evolution is screws, nuts, and bolts of a house that is the naturalistic view of the world—a view of the world in which God does not exist. The foundation of this house is the desire to explain the world without the presence God. *Why would anyone want a worldview devoid of the presence of God?* If there is no God, then there is no one to be held accountable to, and therefore we (humans) are the masters of our destiny—we become our own god.

It is well known that Charles Darwin is credited with proposing an explanation to describe the process by which diversity in life arose. Basically, new varieties of organisms are the result of the struggle to exist; those with differing traits over time will out-compete those with traits less fit to their environment and therefore produce more of their own kind. That is true, that is observable, and that actually fits just fine with a biblical world view. Darwin called this process *natural selection*. Others deemed it *micro evolution*. Many creationists just call it *variation*.

Applying this idea as a means to explain how we went from amoeba to australopithecine is called *macroevolution,* and it is not observable and never will be. In fact, we have never observed any species evolving into a new and different species. Professor at Michigan State Richard E. Lenski leads a well-known long-term (over twenty-eight years) study of E. coli—one of the most quickly reproducing organisms on the planet. For sixty-five thousand (and counting) bacterial generations under selective pressure, many variations have been produced, but these bacteria have not ceased being bacteria.

A turning point in my understanding of evolution came after watching a video entitled *Creatures That Defy Evolution.* This video showed an example of the flagellum motor (the part of a bacteria that causes a flagellum to move). After studying more about this biological machine, I learned it is made up of interlocking parts each dependent on one another to function. It has a propeller, rotor, stator, sensors, and more. This is only one tiny part of a singled cell organism!

This organism is extraordinarily complex—all living organisms are! From observing this complexity, I decided that a process determined by chance could not have caused the precise placement of the proteins, amino acids, and DNA sequences.

Let's say I take an object like an engine apart and remove every sprocket, every spring, and every bolt and place them in a giant box. Let's say I'm incredibly strong and can lift this box and shake it around for fifteen minutes. Do you think the engine parts inside the box will come together to form an engine capable of functioning? Absolutely not.

If I shook it for a year, do you think it would put itself together? No. If I shook it for fifty years, could it put itself together? (Here is where the confusion sets in.) *Well maybe a couple pieces*, one might think. If I shook it for a million years, could this engine put itself together? *Gee, that's a long time … it's possible. Wrong!* This is an inanimate object and only one part of the car! Imagine trying to add all the parts of the car plus the necessary oil, gas, water, and other fluids to the mix! No matter how long you shake that box full of automobile parts and vital fluids, you will never get a fully functioning automobile! How could this logic ever be applied to something as complex as a living organism?

That is essentially what the evolutionist wants you to believe. According to them, earth was a fireball that cooled for millions and millions of years and became a hot rock. Vast amounts of water appeared, then it began to rain on the rock for millions and millions of years more. A "soup" of water and elements began to put themselves together and make proto-cells, the proto-cells formed actual cells, the cells began to form multicellular colonies (fast forward millions and millions of more years), life left the sea, plants formed, animals formed, and we formed.

The evolution of the first cell is something that is virtually a mathematical impossibility! In fact, over thirty years ago, astronomer and cosmologist Sir Fred Hoyle calculated the probability of forming the first cell out of the primordial yuck evolutionists believe life spontaneously generated from. He came up with a 1 in $10^{40,000}$ chance of this happening. It's been estimated that there are approximately 10^{80} atoms in the known universe. That number is enormous! Therefore the probability of a cell forming itself spontaneously is infinitely microscopic, pretty much impossible without the intervention of a Creator!

Many scientist will go as far as to believe that creator to be some alien race. However, one would still have to explain how that alien race came to be. As an infinite and eternal being, God as described in the Holy Bible did not have a beginning- He just is and always was. He is the uncaused first cause.

Complex living, breathing organisms are made up of perfectly interwoven tissues, organs, and networks of electro-chemical impulses so precisely wired that we are capable of sensing and responding to the world around us. What a miracle! Humans are even equipped with the hardware that allows us to sense this world and realize that we are part of it and connected to something beyond it. Evolution did not put us together. A loving and intelligent Creator (who we are made in the image of) created us, this world, and all that is in it!

Enjoying some painting at home.

*Live painting during a Memorial Day art show
at River's Edge Gallery in Kerrville, TX.*

CHAPTER 11

Wanting More

Through my research, I came across so many great books, websites, videos, and other resources that dive much deeper into the subject of apologetics and creation science. I now knew without a shadow of a doubt that there was room in my reality for an all-powerful God that created everything, everywhere, and everyone, both the seen and the unseen. It's a real awakening spiritually and mentally when you realize this. I had to come to grips with how I was living this life. When I realized that there will be a day I will face my maker, it was as though a gift was given to me. This was a new opportunity to start over again.

Armed with research and rediscovered faith, I decided that I needed to tell the world what

I found. I thought the best way I could do this was with a presentation. I started to put my ideas down and constructed a presentation on my computer. The information was good and true but not organized. The only one who could understand what I was trying to say was me! I had to painfully explain every slide to those I shared it with. What I wanted to present had no flow or organization. It was as though a pool of facts and debatable concepts exploded onto a screen. I wasn't trained in this area of study like a teacher or a professor. I needed help! Like any normal red-blooded man, I don't like to ask for help. So I pressed on, knowing somewhere down the line I would run into some resource or someone who could assist.

Another year went by, and rather than pursuing my presentation, I filled my time with painting on canvas instead. Painting was a great therapy tool, and I realized I still had this skill I could put to work. Despite gaining some notoriety through painting, I felt an incessant tug in my spirit to share my supernatural encounters and the creation science information I learned. Many of my friends during his time were not very impressed with my discoveries—just my art.

It's a paradoxical experience to be surrounded by people but feel like you are alone—speaking with others but not really communicating with anyone. I longed for some companionship—someone interested in discussing scientific and spiritual ideas, someone I could engage in a discussion with. One fateful day I met that person—and she happened to be the love of my life.

CHAPTER 12
꠸ ꠹
The Help Mate

A friend of mine invited me to come out with her to a surprise birthday party. I did not expect to meet my future wife there. Like any single guy would do, I looked over the women in the room, but nobody really caught my eye. Then she walked in, with a big smile on her face. She said, "Hi!" We recognized each other through the scattered pages of social media. She had organized this soiree and was a mutual friend—my best friend's, friend's best friend. We all found a table, and I turned on the charm. I was making everyone laugh and carrying on. It was a karaoke party, so I of course had to show off yet another one of my talents.

She sang a song to her friend for her birthday, and it was very sweet. I thought, *Wow, she really loves her friend! I wonder if she could love me like that.* So I did what any sane person would do. I recorded her. She sang like a punk rock angel. I was immediately smitten and wanted to know more. I finally got enough courage and calmly walked up to the stage and picked my song. Thank God, they had it in the selection! I am convinced that my whole life would have been different if they had not had that song. I waited for my entry—the sound of the first chorus. When it began, I belted out the first words and sang my heart out! It was as though the whole bar stopped and all eyes were on me. The song seemed like it went on forever. Finally, it came to an end, and the roar of applause began. Mission accomplished! She finally gave me the attention I deserved.

She slid her chair close to mine and asked, "So you're an artist?" I knew she had a science background and overheard that she worked for an environmental firm, so I quipped, "You're a scientist?" She smiled. We started talking, and we got close and tried to have a conversation, but it was too loud. It got late, and everybody decided to call it a night. She casually suggested that the group go out the next Friday to an art festival. I said to myself, *Yeah She likes me.*

That whole week I tried to play it as cool as I could on social media. I didn't log on too much, and when I did post, my messages were concise. I was cool on the outside but jumping up and down like a school girl at a Beatles concert on the inside. That week as I awaited for our next meeting, the sun shined a little brighter, the air was a little softer, and the birds chirped a little sweeter.

Friday finally came around, and we all confirmed our group date. My friend Vic was the first to show up. I told him I was going to look for her. She kept calling me to find out where I was and if I had found the place alright. She saw me through the crowd while I was still on the phone with her. We greeted with a smile and an embrace. Our group began the art walk—the streets were filled with canvas, metal work, prints, frames, and even performance art. We talked about the pieces as we weaved in and out of studios. We gravitated to each other; it was as though as no one else was around. We simply enjoyed one another's company.

After the art walk, we all went dancing and later to a friend's house. We stayed up talking to one another, literally until the sun came up. I told her about everything: my hometown and family, army life and the fateful day in Afghanistan, and also my near-death experiences. We both discussed that we were looking for a serious relationship and were tired of the dating games many played at our age. It really was a match made in heaven, a miracle! We got married three months later.

My new and true love, my partner in life.

In awe of God bringing us two together.

When the honeymoon was over, we started discussing our views on evolution and creation. We debated for months and months. You have to understand something—my wife was a bookworm brainiac her whole school life. She took a lot of pride and found her identity in her scholastic accomplishments. She was extremely interested in the sciences, namely molecular biology. She studied biology at our local state university and later traveled to California to study at Stanford University. She was a high school biology teacher for six years and had interned in a medical research institute. My point is, she was immersed in and enthralled by the sciences. To her, evolution was not debatable; it was an indisputable fact.

Through her many years of science training in secular institutions, she had learned to not question what she was being taught. *What's the harm in presenting students with facts that support the evolutionary theory as well as facts that support a creation theory?* She often wondered. That idea was vehemently shut down by her education professor while in grad school. She was basically told that it was not appropriate and basically illegal to lend teaching time to theories other than evolution while in a classroom setting.

True and honest science is having the freedom to examine the strengths and weaknesses of all the available evidence and develop the strongest possible explanation (theory). When new reliable evidence threatens the initial theory, we should have the right to explore the evidence and possibly reconsider the original theory. Unfortunately, today we are limited to explore evidence only within the confines of evolution.

The movie *Expelled: No Intelligence Allowed*, starring Ben Stein, documents the fact that not all scientists are on board with Darwinian evolution as the ultimate answer to the origins question. Also noted in the documentary are negative impacts on the careers and educational experiences of people in academia that disagree with the prevailing evolutionary view.

Believe it or not, the debate is not over. As of February 8, 2017, The Discovery Institute's "A Scientific Dissent From Darwinism" displayed the names of over nine hundred PhD-trained scientists from around the world that have openly signed a statement professing the following:

> We are skeptical of claims for the ability of random mutation and natural selection to account for the complexity of life. Careful examination of the evidence for Darwinian theory should be encouraged.
> —*A Scientific Dissent from Darwinism (dissentfromdarwin.org)*

After presenting my wife with creation science information, she really started to question her worldview. It was time for her to make a choice. She finally concluded that I was right. Everything she had been taught and everything she taught was built on a lie—a lie that for many has the power to shape a totally godless worldview. However, she was not godless. She had a relationship with God. She spoke with Him daily, read her Bible, and was even active in her local church. She just always thought, or somewhere along the line was taught, that supernatural and natural things must be separated.

There was no room for God ideas in the science classroom. Those ideas were private, not to be discussed, and could in no way be mixed with the process of science. She reconciled her private life as a Christian and her public life as a science educator by believing that God used evolution to shape and create the world we see.

In her case, God was not allowed to penetrate all areas of her life. This led her to leave God out of many things. God was left out of her recreational drinking habit. He was left out of her relationships with other people. He was left out of her music, her language, and where she chose to spend her time.

When we lead lives with God kept in a safe little box that we only open on Sunday mornings, or when we need something from Him, He is not real to us. He can't give us the victory in our lives we so desperately need. She lived years, as many people do, losing to anxiety, depression, and fear. Once she realized that Jesus is our Creator, not just our Savior, she really began to understand what a vast and mighty God He is.

Her relationship with Him went to a whole new level. Conviction rooted and growth took hold, like a tree planted near water. Her life has amazingly transformed since then. The Lord took away her dependence on alcohol, she has more joy and peace, and she has a hope that is stronger than the obstacles we've faced as a family. The Lord is not done yet. We have only just begun. In 2012 we developed an evangelism presentation, which included our testimonies and creation science information. We began sharing the information we found in churches and schools across Texas and on our website, howiknow.org.

Today, our lives have a new purpose. I continue to paint and share my testimony anywhere I'm invited. My wife provides the necessary support and organization in the background to make it all possible. God also recently blessed us with a new addition to our family, and we have many aspirations for the future.

Sharing our testimonies and my art at
First Baptist Church- Broaddus, TX

Thankful for the opportunities to share the Gospel with others.

A new and bright future for my family. Life is worth living!

67

CHAPTER 13

New Life

Being born in America is a huge advantage in the spiritual sense. Let us not forget that this country began with the Pilgrims' desire to freely live a life based on what they had learned in the Bible. If you take the time to research the Pilgrims' journey, their escape from persecution, and their struggle to survive those first years, you'll find it's truly a miracle that America was ever born. Today we have easy access to Christianity like no other people in all of history. Christianity today has educational institutions, scholars, and numerous books on Christian thought and philosophy. We have the liberty to practice our religion freely, unlike Jesus's original disciples. Modern people in America have access to truth, yet we squander it. It is cheap to us, and worthless to some. I've been guilty of taking it for granted also.

The journey back to Christ is so simple and accessible now. I did not have to backpack through Europe or the Middle East to find the original birthplace of civilization. I did not have to dig through the sands of time to unearth an ancient scroll that was hidden from the rest of the world. I did not have to scale the cold, snowy mountains of Tibet to find a monk to explain life to me or the depravity of the human condition. All I had to do was look in the Good Book. God will not force us into a relationship with Him. Every moment He offers us the right to choose to follow Him—a God-given free will.

Choosing to surrender control of what we think is our life to a God we cannot physically see or touch, and believing there is a God that we will someday face is frightening to consider. It's equally frightening to choose to believe that there is no God and we exist on a planet that spins over one thousand miles per hour traveling at a speed over sixty-six thousand miles per hour around a giant ball of flames, the sun. My search for truth—truth that fits physical evidence, and the metaphysical such as morality, justice, freedom, and the existence of miracles—has led me to a genuine relationship with the one true God: Jesus.

I've been reborn. I have a new way of thinking, a new way of speaking, and a new way of acting. I'm not perfect and won't be until the Lord perfects me on that faithful day. However, I have a hope that many desire to have. They may not even realize it yet, but they desperately need it.

The truth is, we are all born broken. Our sin separates us from God. As we become more separated from Him, we feel the pull, the aching feeling in the pit of our soul that something is not yet complete. We may try to fill it with acceptance from a relationship, money, status in society, honors, substances, and other idols. We will never be filled and free until we let the truth of Jesus set us free from the bondage of sin. Of all the figures in the major religious worldviews (Judeo-Christian, Islamic, and Buddhist), Jesus didn't claim to know the truth, He told us he is *the Truth*. "I am the way, the truth, and the life. No one can come to the Father except through me" (John 14:6 NLT).

Christianity recognizes that all have sinned

and have fallen short of God's glorious standard. If we think we are without sin or can somehow earn our way to heaven, we are fooling ourselves!

> God saved you by his grace when you believed. And you can't take credit for this; it is a gift from God. Salvation is not a reward for the good things we have done, so none of us can boast about it. For we are God's masterpiece. He has created us anew in Christ Jesus, so we can do the good things he planned for us long ago. (Ephesians 2:8–10 NLT)

God promises in the Bible that no matter where you have been or what you did in your past, He will forgive you and accept you. God's desire is to be in relationship with you. Jeremiah 29 says that when we look for Him with all our heart, He promises that we will find Him. As you abide in Him and He in you, you will bear the fruit of a new life in Christ.

If you are reading this story today and you are truly ready to enter a relationship with your

Creator, it's simple. His word says in Romans 10:9–13 that If you confess with your mouth that Jesus Christ is Lord and believe in your heart that God raised Him from the dead, you will be saved.

As you draw near to Him, He will draw near to you. Begin to read the Bible and grow in your faith. Other resources to strengthen your faith are available on our website howiknow.org. It is my sincere prayer that you grow in the fullness of the Lord and knowledge of Him and that you will be blessed with all spiritual blessings in Christ Jesus.

Little Sins

My soul feels like it's in a drought. My little sin keeps me from my Lord, the spring of living water.

My little sin makes me question: Does He really see me? Can the cloak of the night cover me from His view? Can the weight of the waters in the deep abyss keep me from His knowledge from such a little thing? Would He even care about this little sin?

If He came back at this very moment, would He take me with Him? If the trumpets blew right now, would I hear them? Why do I do this? Did He make me like this? Who am I really hurting? I am not as bad as so and so. Surely there are worse Christians in the world, right? Enough! Excuses! This guilt is *not* too heavy to quit, but heavy and burdensome enough to hurt. I feel like a fake. How can I look people straight in the roundness of their eyes? Well, I have been assured that there are no perfect people on this earth. So … there! I can sleep better to night.

No! No! No! Who can I blame for this little sin? Can I blame my past? Can I blame my present? The future seems to be my only friend, but I know she will let me down, in the midst of the perfect storm. Something needs to change. I try and I try, but with no success. I know the Sunday school answer to all my questions—Jesus—but He seems so far at times. When I am on the mountaintop, He is there holding my hand. Then I get into a valley, and I feel like He is nowhere to be found. Where did you go, my Lord?

Then I realize it is I who left. He refused to walk in the unnecessary, unholy valley. He begged for me to stay on the high road, but I listened to my flesh, completely distracted. We, my flesh and I, walked down entertained among the jagged rocks, down into the pit where nightmares lurk and scheme. My flesh has sold me out! I am not where I want to be!

I get trapped and beg my Messiah to help me out of this trammel, this decoy, this snare.

How long will you help me with the same little sin? I ask Him, "Will my righteousness ever run out?" Twice I utter the Sunday school answer. No it will not! Cleanse me, Lord! I want to be in right standing with You again! Forgive me! When will I ever be completely holy, without sin? Three times I have a Sunday school answer. Never! As long as I walk in this corruptible flesh vestment.

Oh, what a wretched man I am. That You, my Lord, had to step out of heaven to become my perfect sacrifice for my little sins and my big ones. Ironically, they are all the same to you. There was never a chance I could attain enough righteousness to not be cast into hell separated from an all-powerful, living God. You, my Savior, broke Your body on the vertical altar we call the cross. You, my Savior, spilled Your blood on the earth from whence I came. Save me from Yourself, the awesome, powerful God who does not change. See me how You see Christ!

Jesus, I pray, help me every day to be more like You. Pick me up when I fall, though there will be many. My loving, thoughtful Creator, Jesus Christ. Amen.

-Mario Lopez

Printed in the United States
By Bookmasters